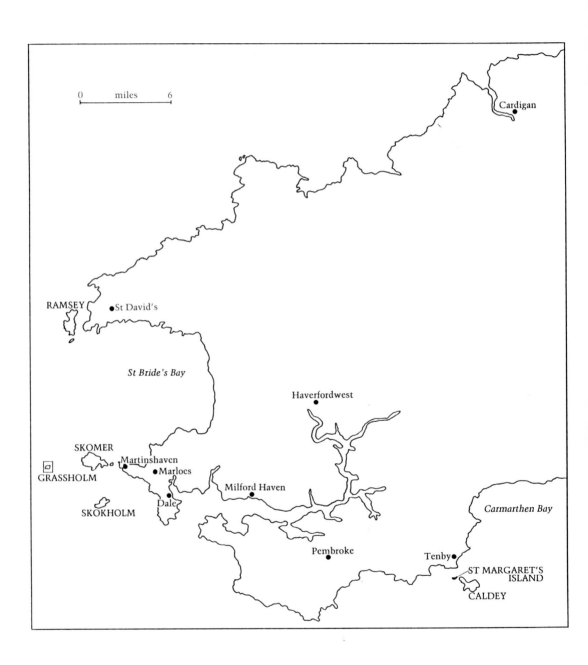

0   miles   6

Cardigan

RAMSEY   •St David's

St Bride's Bay

Haverfordwest

SKOMER

Martinshaven

GRASSHOLM   •Marloes

Milford Haven

Carmarthen Bay

SKOKHOLM   •Dale

Pembroke

Tenby•

ST MARGARET'S ISLAND

CALDEY

Pembrokeshire's Islands

Roscoe Howells

First Impression—September 1994
Second Impression—July 1997

ISBN 1 85902 122 0

*Printed by J. D. Lewis and Sons Ltd.,
Gomer Press, Llandysul, Dyfed, Wales.*

CONTENTS

1   Introduction   7

2   Nineteenth-century Skomer and Skokholm   8

3   Nineteenth-century Ramsey and Grassholm   14

4   Nineteenth-century Caldey   17

5   Twentieth-century Skomer and Skokholm   20

6   Twentieth-century Ramsey   23

7   Twentieth-century Caldey   26

8   Natural History   29

1   Introduction

Not taking into account the islets and those which are insular only at high tide, there are five Pembrokeshire islands which have been inhabited at one time or another.

They are Caldey (or Ynys Bŷr, in Welsh) and St Margaret's to the south, Skomer and Skokholm to the west, and Ramsey (or Ynys Dewi) to the north-west. Then there is Grassholm, far out in the Atlantic, which, although never inhabited, has played some small part in the island story.

Apart from any occupation by the early Celtic people, and any early religious settlements, man's interest in the islands has always been agricultural plus, to a much lesser extent, exploitation of the seabirds. Even on Caldey, where there was a second religious occupation of the island, with a settlement of Benedictine monks for the four hundred years from 1131 to the dissolution of the monasteries in 1535, there was agricultural activity.

The Scandinavian names were probably given to the islands as places which were little more than landmarks. From those times up to the late eighteenth century their equable climate would have made them particularly suitable to support the mainly subsistence farming which was also practised on the mainland. Little would have been needed by way of herding and shepherding.

One particular feature of the islands' economy was their suitability for the breeding of rabbits which had been introduced about 1300. In the absence of natural predators, rabbits thrived and were a highly profitable crop. Because they were the property of the landlord there are numerous figures in Crown records to show the number and cash value of the seasonal catches.

The latter half of the eighteenth century saw a great improvement in farming techniques and this, coupled with the effect of the Napoleonic wars and the subsequent high prices, led to a steep increase in rents. Part of the prosperity was due to the increase in corn-growing occasioned both by the effect of the wars and of the duty on imported corn. The inevitable recession after the wars led to a collapse in prices, but the high rents remained. Apart from the occasional good year there was no great joy for the farming community from 1815 to 1853, during which period there was also a series of exceptionally wet seasons.

From the middle of the nineteenth century onwards there was a marked improvement in the farming economy. Much of this, however, was the result of the coming of the railways which now brought the prosperous industrial areas of south Wales within striking distance of those with fat lambs, beef and dairy produce to sell, even from as far west as Pembrokeshire. And this is where the similarity which had for centuries existed between the island and the mainland farming can be seen to have taken different roads.

Between the islands and the mainland were stretches of water, often treacherous, which had to be negotiated by boats carrying requisites to the islands and, also, perhaps more importantly, transporting the produce to the mainland. Apart from the vagaries of the markets from time to time, these extra costs were an intolerable burden in an age when business was becoming increasingly cost conscious, to say nothing of the times when stock, which had been fattened for market, had to be kept on the islands for days, and sometimes weeks on end because of adverse weather conditions.

Whilst these factors applied to all the islands in general, there was one distinction between Caldey and the other three islands of Skomer, Skokholm and Ramsey. On each of the three western islands, apart from anything that had happened in the earliest years of history, there was only ever the one farm and its household of family and servants, whereas on Caldey there had always been a community. As far back as the Dissolution, for example, in addition to the small monastery, there were no fewer than nine tenants there.

In addition to the farming on Caldey there was, for much of the nineteenth century, a thriving quarrying industry with up to 20,000 tons of limestone being exported annually.

The export of quarried limestone, Caldey.

Indeed, at one time, lime was being burned on the island and exported. There were two lime-kilns on the island, and there were also kilns on Ramsey, Skomer and Skokholm. The lime was used for fertiliser, and also as the basis for the mortar and plaster when building had to be done.

Whereas at one time the islands of the west coast, apart from Ramsey, had all been in the possession of Charles Philipps of Sandyhaven and Haythog, in 1740 the ownership of Skokholm had passed to William Allen of Gelliswick and later of Dale Castle. It has remained in the possession of Dale Castle since that time.

By the beginning of the nineteenth century Skomer was owned by William Charles Allen Philipps of St Brides. There were various tenants during the earlier part of the century but, for one short period, Philipps was in occupation and, in keeping with the times, he carried out great improvements to the house and farm buildings which included a fine new range of stables and cattle-sheds with lofts above them. In the roofing, full use was made of timber from the great wooden masts of old sailing ships wrecked upon this treacherous coast.

Late in the 1840s Skomer was let to an Edward Robinson. A widower with three young children, a son and two daughters, he was the son of a London merchant who lived near Romford in Essex, and he had studied agriculture in Essex and Norfolk. He was quick to see that the rabbit catch could be sufficient to pay the rent, and one of the first things he did was to set men to topping the outside boundary walls with heather to confine the rabbits to the outer areas of the island. In the previous century the field system had been laid out by using the stones of earlier Celtic settlements, enclosing about three hundred acres of the island's seven hundred odd acres. The records show catches of 6,000 to 8,000 rabbits a season.

Amongst other more orthodox farming

activities he established a herd of red deer and also a flock of pure-bred Cochin-China fowls. In 1859, Robinson's daughter Annie, unmarried and living at home, wrote to her sister, Ellen, and said,

> Papa wishes very much that Vaughan would be good enough to try and get some large Malay fowls & bring home when you come. He wants the heaviest birds, not those with long legs and small bodies. If you can manage to bring home some fine cocks & hens he will be very much pleased & obliged.
>
> We have a swarm of poultry, more than 100, mostly ducks. My geese eggs were all failures.

Robinson did well on Skomer, living in some style and entertaining shooting parties from time to time, breeding some pheasants and partridges. There were also hares on the island at that time and, of course, there were wild-duck on the two ponds, as well as snipe and many migratory woodcock in season. As was the custom of the times he also shot many rare birds for mounting in glass cases.

As far as his farming was concerned it has to be said that he was fortunate in going into the island when the financial tide was about to start running in his favour. Then, in 1861, he was followed by his son-in-law, Captain Vaughan Palmer Davies, who had married Robinson's daughter, Ellen. Captain Davies and his family were to remain on Skomer for thirty years and their occupation must be one of the most memorable of all the island stories. It is certainly one of the best chronicled.

Vaughan Davies was born at Broomhill, near Dale, went to sea, and at an early age was commanding sailing-clippers trading between Bombay, Calcutta and Hong Kong. One of the ships was named *The Arrow* and it was at this time that Annie wrote asking that Vaughan should bring back some Malay fowls. A considerable part of the clippers' trade involved the carying of opium, much to the displeasure of the Chinese government, since it led to the degradation of the Chinese people. On one occasion Vaughan's sister, Emily, wrote to him and, having expressed some disquiet over the dangers of the trade in which he was involved, went on to say,

> . . . nor am I quite satisfied of the lawfulness of the trade in opium. I don't understand the matter myself but so many of the best people I know think it wrong . . .

In 1857 the second of the Opium wars was started when a ship called *The Arrow*, and flying the British flag, was seized by the 'heathen Chinese'. It is not known whether Vaughan Davies's ship was *The Arrow* involved.

Finally, disillusioned and sickened by the duplicity of his employers, he returned to England and was looking for another ship when Robinson persuaded him to take over his lease on Skomer.

The many family letters show Captain Davies to have been a man of strong Christian conviction and, to the end of his time on Skomer, as he had done on board ship, he conducted prayers each morning before breakfast and held a service on Sunday. To read these letters, and some of his wife's diaries which have survived, is to have a marvellous insight into the way of life and the attitudes of the age. Not least of the interesting references is to the custom of smoking the hams and bacon in the smoking oven, probably of seventeenth- or eighteenth-century date, which remained in pristine

The bacon-smoking oven alongside the so-called Flemish chimney, Skomer.

condition until it was vandalised by more recent occupiers.

Through generations the boatmen who served the island were the Edwards family of Marloes. To communicate with them Captain Davies had a tall flagstaff, which had once been a ship's mast, and this was anchored to the Spy Rock in a field near the house, where the iron fastenings remained until recently. The hoisting of one heather bush indicated to the boatmen that they were needed. Two bushes told them to bring the blacksmith and three meant that the doctor was needed.

Then there are the many references to the difficulties which bad weather could engender, particularly when cattle or sheep were due to

The Skomer boatmen.

go to the fair, as markets were then called, or when poultry which had been killed, feathered and dressed were due to go off at Christmas. Added to this was the fact that farming fortunes had again taken a turn for the worse towards the end of the 1870s when arable farming declined rapidly. A series of wet harvests coinciding with a flood of grain imports from overseas, plus the mounting costs of farm labour, resulted in arable land being turned back to pasture. But from the mid 1880s onwards meat and dairy produce brought in from abroad in the new refrigerated steamships dealt a crippling blow to the home producer.

During that time Skokholm had become vacant and Vaughan Davies rented it for the grazing of ponies, red deer and sheep, as well as for the trapping of rabbits. And he literally 'kept an eye' on his stock there by means of his powerful spy-glass, a relic of his seafaring days. This tenancy, too, came to an end when he left Skomer in the spring of 1892. He was sixty-six years of age at the time. Only two attempts were to be made to farm Skomer after that, and only one attempt to farm Skokholm.

Although Skokholm has some good soil, being smaller and less accessible than Skomer or Ramsey it never compared with them as an agricultural entity. In 1760 a new house was built, together with farm buildings,

The tall flagstaff anchored to the Spy Rock, Skomer.

An aerial view of Skokholm.

The farm on Skokholm.

and about half of the island's two hundred acres round the farmstead were walled in.

During the Napoleonic wars the rent rose very quickly to £100 per annum. Remaining at that figure when the years of depression followed, it meant that Skokholm became an unattractive proposition for anyone thinking of farming it. Richard Fenton (1747-1821), author of *A Historical Tour through Pembrokeshire* (1810), had some interesting observations to make, including the oft-quoted statement by John Lloyd that the house had been 'built after a whimsical manner, which has a small beast-house and a dairy, with stables besides'.

During the first half of the century the indications are that Skokholm was being farmed by a mainland farmer with the farm servants living on the island. Usually, Martinshaven, the beach beyond Marloes, was the point of embarkation for both islands

but, in 1851, Skokholm was being farmed
from Dale by a James Davies of The Hooks, a
farm near that village. By 1861 Davies had
only two women on the island, a 'house and
dairy maid' and her 'assistant'. In all prob-
ability their work would have been to milk
the cows and make butter which would have
been fetched in tubs from time to time.

James Davies was drowned, along with a
boy named James Roberts, when crossing to
the island in 1862, and soon afterwards it was
rented by Captain Henry Edward Harrison. A
native of Waterston, near Milford, he had
skippered a boat sailing with copper ore from
Cuba to Swansea where he and his family
then lived.

During his tenure of the 'lower' island, as
Skokholm was referred to by the Marloes
fishermen, farming was prosperous, but his
own activities were on nothing like the scale
of the retired sea-captain on the neighbouring
'upper' island of Skomer. In 1870, for example,
the Agricultural Returns show that there
were four cows in-milk, eleven other cattle

Martha Jane Warlow.

and four horses. Only one man was regularly
employed and, in spite of the agricultural
prosperity, only enough corn to feed the
stock was being grown. This would have
been threshed by hand flail on the floor of the
barn. On Skomer there were two horse-
courses to power the in-barn thresher and the
chaff-cutter, winnowing machine and root
pulper.

Captain Harrison died on Skokholm in
1881 at the age of sixty-six and fires were lit
to attract attention from the mainland. One
of his grand-daughters, the late Mrs Martha
Jane Warlow, at the age of ninety-two
recalled coming out from the island in the
boat and sitting on her grandfather's coffin
and the men rowing. That night she was put
to sleep in an old-fashioned cupboard-bed in
one of the cottages to which the women
usually came from the two islands for their
confinements.

It was following this that Captain Vaughan
Palmer Davies took over the tenancy of
Skokholm for a time.

Captain Henry Edward Harrison.

The farmhouse, buildings and hayricks, Skomer, 1889.

During the nineteenth century much the same sort of farming activities were taking place on Ramsey. Both on Ramsey and Skomer there remained traces of the old five-step ploughing as a legacy of the great corn era of the Napoleonic wars. And it is of further interest that, for a period during those hostilities, both islands were held by a John Summers, who lived at Moor in the parish of Walwyn's Castle. Ramsey was held on lease from the Bishop of St David's, the bishops having held the island from the earliest times.

Under his will, dated 24 July 1816, Summers left his leasehold interest in Ramsey to his son, William Bowlas Summers, and after him, should he die under age, to his other son, James Bowlas Summers. These boys were at that time aged nine and seven, respectively.

In 1822 William's trustees granted a lease on Ramsey to John Evans of Mabus in the parish of Mathry and it is clear that he did a great deal of work there. Ten years later William Bowlas Summers, who had now come of age, brought an action in the High Court of Chancery for this lease to be set aside and for possession of the island to be given to him. This action was successful and, after all due compensation had been allowed to John Evans for his improvements, Summers was granted a new lease for three lives in September 1832 at the yearly rent of £8 6s 6d. He died three years later at the age of twenty-eight and the various properties and leases passed to his brother, James.

Across the years, almost up to the present day, Ramsey has been the source of much contention and litigation, and the pattern, which had already been set, continued with

The farm and farm buildings, Ramsey.

the occupation of the island by a Thomas Morse, of Hayscastle parish, whose financial dealings with his wife's brother, Levi Griffith of Rickeston, have been dealt with extensively in *The Sounds Between* (1968) and shed interesting light on agricultural customs and prices of the day. Amongst other things it shows that John Summers was making an extortionate profit on the rent he was paying the Bishop. In the 1850s, when farming fortunes were on the mend, he again began farming the island himself. In 1860 he let the island on lease for three lives to Thomas Llewellin of Lower Treginnis.

'Squire Llewellin', as he was known, continued to farm on the mainland, but by 1867 had relinquished the tenancy of Ramsey to William Williams, a merchant, of The Grove, St David's. As well as having a lime, coal and corn merchant's business on the mainland he and his wife also kept the public house, The Grove Hotel. They, too, continued to live on the mainland and farmed Ramsey with a bailiff. Mrs Williams was a woman of tremendous resilience and determination, and she it was who was mainly responsible for the island farming.

Water from a pond powered a corn-mill with an overshot wheel and, as on Skomer, there was a horse-course. There was also accommodation for six horses and eighty head of horned stock, including twenty-four cows, and also piggeries. Most of these improvements would no doubt have been carried out earlier by John Evans.

As well as the traditional farming there are many other details of passing interest which have come to light, such as the fact that the Williams' bred angora rabbits on the rock next to the one known as the Axe so that they could have bucks which they turned loose on the island to improve the strain. They also fed calves on a custard made from the eggs of the eligugs, a corruption of *heligog*, the Welsh word for guillemots, but which in this case no doubt also included razorbills.

The Williams' were followed for a short time, through dark and desparate days for the farming community, by their son-in-law Luther Bowen Rees, and the island was sold by the Ecclesiastical Commissioners in 1904 to Wynford Philipps, who later took the title Lord St David's.

William Williams, The Grove, St David's.

Out in the Atlantic, eight miles to the west of Skomer, twenty-two acre Grassholm had some small place in the overall pattern. Appearing long ago in the Mabinogion as Gwales in Penfro, the island later caught the poetic imagination of the great Cardiff naturalist, Robert Drane, who wrote of it in 1895:

> It is at once so near, and yet so remote: so weird, and blank, and solitary, yet still within the kingdom of mankind. So barren and inhospitable, yet so secure and compassable, primitive and free, that it becomes at once, one's own estate in fee.

There is much evidence to suggest that sheep were grazed on the island in the Middle Ages. Possibly this became a less attractive proposition in an age which saw the depredations of pirates round the coastal areas but it is known that sheep were kept there at various times throughout the nineteenth century when the Marloes fishermen also used to spend many nights on Grassholm when they

Part of the huge breeding colony of gannets, Grassholm.

were fishing for lobsters in the days of oar and sail. The remains of a stone compound on the higher ground serve as a reminder of the days when wethers were kept on the island and shepherded mainly for shearing in an age when wool was of prime value.

Today, however, Grassholm is renowned for its huge breeding colony of gannets. Time was when there were thousands of puffins there, but these are no longer to be seen on the island which has been virtually taken over by the great white solan geese with their six-foot wing span. This change has come about in not much more than the last hundred years.

It is thought that gannets first settled on Grassholm following persecution of the old Lundy colony by channel pilots and other egg stealers, which eventually resulted in the birds abandoning their former colony altogether. Present-day writers have suggested various dates and figures for the colonisation of Grassholm, but the most reliable and authentic show that the dozen pairs in 1872 had increased to 300 pairs by 1905. By 1964 there were estimated to be 15,500 pairs and

more then 30,000 in 1988. If there is some variation in numbers recorded during the years when the colony was becoming established up until the time of the First World War, it must be remembered that the birds, their eggs and their young were frequently subjected to the most awful and senseless persecution in the name of sport. For example, in a letter dated 1849, we read:

Last Tuesday week I went in company with your brothers & Co to Grassholm —we got there about 11.0 o'clock P.M. and Harry and myself waged an incessant war with the puffins &c &c until we left which was not before 4 o'clock the next day.

A similar well publicised incident took place in 1890. Perhaps such behaviour was not too surprising in an age when people cut the wings from living birds for use as adornments to women's hats, and cold-bloodedly threw the mutilated birds into the sea to struggle until a lingering death came to their relief. The Sea Birds Protection Act of 1869 eventually put a stop to this barbarity.

An aerial view of Caldey.

Thomas Kynaston of Pembroke.

Life on Caldey was rather different. It has already been noted that there has always been a community on Caldey, and never was this more pronounced than throughout the nineteenth century.

In 1792 the island was bought by Thomas Kynaston of Pembroke who built a mansion adjoining the mediaeval priory. When he died in 1812 he was succeeded by his twenty-year old son, Cabot, who was to remain on the island until his death in 1866. He it was who developed the quarrying industry on Caldey. In an age when it was difficult, because of the system of parish relief, for workers to move from one parish to another, it is fascinating to see how those who lived on Caldey had hailed from all the parishes along the coast from Laugharne in the east to Lamphey in the west. Because of its extra-parochial status, which had obtained from as far back as a grant by Henry I in 1113, the Squire of Caldey maintained his own poor and therefore paid a living wage. In addition there were many workers who went over to the island on a weekly basis. At Christmas time in 1834 fifteen of them were drowned in a fatality off the Scur Rocks when coming home to their families.

For maybe something like fifteen to twenty years around this time Kynaston also carried out quarrying on adjoining St Margaret's, known in earlier times as Little Caldey. As recently as 1810 there had been a 'little chapel' there but this was converted by Kynaston for use as a dwelling and in 1841 there were three families living on the island.

Following the death of Cabot Kynaston, Caldey was bought in 1867 by James Wilson Hawksley for his only son, James Taylor Hawksley, who had studied agriculture at Cirencester. He came in on the crest of the wave when farming was prosperous and spent vast sums on building improvements, machinery and steam-heated greenhouses. He also took an active interest in civic affairs became an alderman of Tenby Borough and High Sheriff of Pembrokeshire in 1884.

In due course Hawksley changed the emphasis of his farming enterprise from livestock breeding to market gardening, and developed between sixty and seventy acres of his land for this purpose. No doubt he found the usual difficulties in crossing livestock to the mainland and sought to circumvent them by exploiting the benign island climate for the growing of vegetables. To this end he purchased a seventy-five ton ketch and she traded between Caldey and such places as Pembroke Dock and Swansea, as well as delivering to Tenby harbour.

Like many others Hawksley, in his later

St Margaret's Island.

years, failed to survive the agricultural slump, and he came to a sad end in 1891. He was followed for a short time by Thomas Dick Smith-Cuninghame who was to leave something of a mark on the island history by introducing the well-known steamer, the twenty ton *Firefly*. After only three years he sold Caldey to the Reverend William Done Bushell. A fine scholar and an all round athlete, he was a Senior Mathematics master at Harrow and, eventually, chaplain and housemaster at that famous public school. He believed that a boy should know something of everything and everything of something. Above all, he was a good man, and a man of God. He spent a great deal of money restoring the island's old ecclesiastical buildings and, with an interest in Anglican monasticism, was responsible for bringing to Caldey in 1906 the Anglican Benedictine monks. This was to have a great bearing on what was to happen on the island throughout the twentieth century and ensure that the story would be quite different from that of the other islands.

Before leaving the nineteenth century it is perhaps of passing interest to note that in 1833 there is reference to Caldey in a case in Chancery involving one Bowlas Summers against James Summers, John Mathias and John Evans. We have already noted their involvement with Skomer and Ramsey around that time, but how their financial affairs would have impinged on Caldey is not known.

The Caldey boat *Firefly*.

Tenby harbour.

Turning to the twentieth century a similar pattern unfolds, more or less, for most of the islands with the exception of Caldey.

Following the departure of Captain Davies, Skomer was farmed for a short time by William Jones of Trehill, and it was during this period that the island was bought by Lord Kensington after more than two centuries in the possession of the Philipps family. Lord Kensington bought it chiefly for the shooting, and this included shooting the seals (to the delight of the fishermen), the pelts being used for making waistcoats, bags and cartridge-belts. Even so, there had by now been an increasing awareness of, and interest in, the islands' wildlife. As far back as July 1857 a newspaper report told of two trains consisting of thirty carriages carrying several hundreds of the inhabitants of the Welsh industrial areas on an excursion to Neyland whence they

subsequently went on a marine trip in the *Malakhoff* off the islands of Skomer and Skokholm, the Smalls Lighthouse in the Irish Channel, the Fortifications at Dale Point, Thorn Island and the Stack Rock. The day, gloomy at its commencement, broke out eventually in unclouded brightness, and the excursionists enjoyed themselves to the top of their bent.

Robert Drane (left foreground) and his friend J. J. Neale (just behind him) with members of the Neale family in Skomer's North Haven.

Reuben and Betty Codd in the company of Walter Sturt (centre).

Reuben Codd, the last man to farm Skomer.

During the short time the Jones family were on Skomer they took paying guests and these included Robert Drane and his friend, J. J. Neale of the Neale and West trawler company. Neale's seven sons all followed in their father's footsteps as first-class naturalists. In 1905 J. J. Neale took a lease on the island and eventually forbade public landing and photography because of the disturbance to the birds. He certainly made a notable contribution in enabling the gannets to become firmly established on Grassholm. With his boys all away at the war, however, he allowed the lease to lapse in 1915 and died four years later.

In 1922 Skomer and its smaller islands, including Grassholm, were bought by Walter Sturt, a retired dentist, who bought the property for the benefit of his wife's health. His daughter subsequently married Reuben Codd, the son of a local farmer and miller. He farmed the island in the years after the Second World War and grew a fine crop of early potatoes in a season when the capricious market of that increasingly popular crop collapsed. Any Pembrokeshire island was the last place on earth for a farmer to be stuck with such a crop on his hands.

After the sale of the island in 1950 Reuben Codd continued to live at Martinshaven, which had long been Skomer's mainland base, and became something of a legend in his own lifetime as he wardened the island for the new owner. Codd was a man of great physical strength, steeped in the lore of the countryside and with a great knowledge of the wild creatures and their ways. The new owner, Leonard Lee, a Midlands industrialist, was prevailed upon in 1959 to sell the island to the Nature Conservancy to be wardened by the West Wales Field Society, and later he admitted to regretting it. As various newspaper reports show, an unhappy time followed and there was no improvement until the chairman and secretary had been removed from office.

In 1937 Walter Sturt, unable to afford the gannets on Grassholm the protection he would have wished, not least in the face of the increasing attention of some of the professional countrymen, had sold the island to M. C. Harman, the owner of Lundy, nearly fifty miles to the south-west. He bought it for his son, J. P. Harman, in the hope that with sufficient protection some of the birds might return to colonise Lundy once again. In 1940 Grassholm was sold to Malcolm Stewart and, through his goodwill, it was acquired by the Royal Society for the Protection of Birds in 1974.

After Captain Davies relinquished the tenancy of Skokholm in 1891 the island was taken for grazing and for the rabbits until John Edwards, better known as 'The Bulldog', went there to farm in 1905 and his farming of the island, until he left in 1912, was perhaps as good as any which Skokholm had ever known. His wife gave birth to their first child there and it was the last birth on any of the western islands. Occuring during a storm, when the young mother was unable to cross to Martinshaven for the confinement as planned, it probably precipitated the decision to leave the island before the birth of their next child.

In 1927 a Cardiff dentist, H. W. Shellard, took the island with his son-in-law, the well-known naturalist R. M. Lockley, who caught the rabbits and wrote a number of books and articles dealing in the main with the seabirds and his own life on the island. He also established the first British bird observatory there in 1933, with the RSPB covering the rent of the island for this purpose. This activity continued after the war when Skokholm was held by the British Council of Field Studies at Dale Fort but when, in the 1960s, a lease was granted to the West Wales Naturalists' Trust, which was the reconstituted West Wales Field Society, there was a stipulation that there was to be no more bird-ringing to interfere with the birds. Likewise on Skomer earlier, the society had to abandon its seal-ringing activities in the face of much criticism of the practice.

Jack 'Bulldog' Edwards, the last man to farm Skokholm.

Ramsey followed the trend towards wildlife awareness to a much lesser extent than the other islands although, with a large colony of Atlantic grey seals coming to its caves and remote pebble beaches to breed in the autumn, and with the colonies of razorbills and guillemots coming to the cliff ledges in spring, there was a quickening of interest on the part of an increasing number of naturalists. Murray Mathew, a keen observer, had left much interesting observation on Ramsey in his *Birds of Pembrokeshire*, published in 1894.

In the first decade of the new century Ramsey was tenanted by the Arnold family of Penarthur, a farm on the mainland, and two of the sons, Ivor and Adrian, both of whom were unmarried at that time, went to live on the island. They were a family with a long sea-going history, as were many of the farming people of the St David's peninsula, and Ivor served with distinction for eighteen years as coxswain for the St David's lifeboat. He also left behind a day-to-day diary which gave a simple and telling insight into life on an off-shore island. Although they were not typical, insofar as they were bachelors for whom their mother or sister would cross to the island occasionally to cook and clean, the notebook is wonderfully revealing of the

Ivor Arnold.

Sheep shearing on Ramsey: Bert Griffiths (left).

Mrs Griffiths making butter in the Ramsey dairy.

loneliness, the interest in the mainland and its people, the thoughts of food and comfort, and the significance of simple little things which mattered to the islanders.

From the time the Arnolds left until the island was bought by Lionel Whitehead in 1935, the succession of tenants was kaleidoscopic, and in assessing their success or failure the state of farming on the mainland at any particular time always had to be kept in mind. Ben Evans, for example, did well there during the First World War, came back to the mainland in 1921 to buy a farm when prices were high and was ruined in the disastrous slump which followed. He then went to Canada where he prospered.

Lionel Whitehead, who was head of the Whitehead Iron and Steel Company, of Abergavenny, bought Ramsey as a birthday present for his wife, Marion. He spent a great deal of money improving the house and farm buildings, and he also provided a landing quay and small harbour by throwing a wall

The new quay, Ramsey, and the Bitches separating the island from the mainland.

across from the island to the rock next to the one known as the Axe. It was brilliantly conceived and a courageous effort which transformed access to the island out of all recognition. Working on the project was one Bert Griffiths, who had been brought up on a farm but had learned his trade as a mason because there was not enough work to keep him at home. He and Lionel Whitehead found themselves with an immediate rapport which resulted in Bert Griffiths becoming the farm manager and subsequently, following the sudden death of the owner, the tenant of the island. After farming there with great success he returned to farm on the mainland, and Ramsey was again farmed by a succession of tenants until it was sold to another wealthy industrialist, K. P. Allpress, who had been a farmer before he became an industrialist.

The intention was to let the island to a farmer with an interest in wildlife and conservation. In practice the idea did not work out. K. P. Allpress was active with the RSPB, was chairman of its Finance Committee,

and had intended that Ramsey should be a nature reserve for all time under the care of that society. Like the other industrialist, Lionel Whitehead, thirty years earlier, he died with tragic suddenness and, for reasons which it would be tedious to chronicle, the RSPB lost their tenure of the island, which again reverted to the more traditional farming pattern of the time.

For a while Ramsey was farmed by Robin Pratt, who had married the daughter of K. P. Allpress, and they established a herd of red deer. Then they moved their farming operations to the mainland and the island was sold to the Henry Sebestyen Trust.

At that stage the farming operations were taken over by John Freeman and his wife, Alison, and they, too, carried on with a herd of red deer. When they left, the island's owners embarked on a scheme which involved appointing wardens and providing a certain amount of self-catering accommodation and facilities for campers, with the island being designated as a Site of Special Scientific Interest. No animals were to be killed.

To those with the slightest knowledge of country matters and the laws of the wild it was evident that such a venture, as a commercial possibility, was bound to fail and, in 1992, Ramsey was sold to the RSPB for an undisclosed sum. The figure of £500,000 which was quoted in the press at the time was said by the society to be 'speculative'.

John and Alison Freeman with their children, Griff and Thomas.

25

The Anglican Benedictines, who came to Caldey in 1906 at the instigation of Done Bushell, subsequently bought the island and built the new monastery between 1910 and 1913. Then they embraced the Catholic faith and, having run into severe financial difficulties, sold the property to the Cistercian Order in 1925. In 1929 the Benedictines moved to Prinknash and the Cistercians sent a contingent of monks from Notre Dame de Scourmont, near Chimay in Belgium, to establish a new foundation. After many vicissitudes, not least the difficulties of foreigners of a silent order trying to establish an English-speaking community, and the colossal interruption of a Second World War when so many of the community were called to serve in the Belgian army, Caldey became autonomous as an Abbey in its own right in 1959.

Living, as they do, according to the Rule of St Benedict, the monks expect to support themselves by their own labours, so that Cistercians are traditionally of agricultural pursuit. They are, however, no more able to make a living farming an off-shore island such as Caldey than anybody else. Their farming, therefore, tends to be geared towards the tourist trade, with the cows in the Jersey herd calving in the spring, so that the milk can go to the tea-rooms on the island throughout the summer season, along with the rest of the dairy produce. The monks have also established a highly successful perfume industry, which is ideally suited to the island economy. The product is easily transportable, with a high value-to-weight ratio, and also easily storable so that it can be made in the off-season winter months and is then on the island ready for sale when the

Caldey Abbey.

The monks at work in the island perfumery.

The community of monks in 1983.

visitors come in the summer. The visitors in the summer season, of course, furnish a considerable portion of the monastic income. Any profit is given to charity. The visitors also contribute appreciably to the local economy in providing employment for the owners and crews of the eleven boats which operate in the Caldey 'pool' throughout the summer season. The monastery's own boat is based in Tenby harbour and runs daily on weekdays throughout the winter.

Of recent years there has been a decline in the number of monastic vocations so that the monks have had to turn increasingly to employed labour to assist them in their commercial ventures. Apart from the monks, Caldey has a resident population of about forty people, including children. There is a school for the younger children, whilst the older ones go to Tenby or Saundersfoot as boarders from Monday to Friday. Unlike the other islands, Caldey is served by mains electricity, which was brought by submarine cable in 1965. The telephone, after an initial experiment with radio telephone in 1951, is also now available by cable which has enabled more of the islanders to benefit from this means of communication.

The guest house on the island accommodates twenty people, and retreats are made there throughout the year, not only by Catholics, but by Christians of all denominations, and indeed by any people of goodwill, whatever their beliefs, if they feel they are likely to derive some benefit from the spirituality they would expect to find on an island where men have devoted their lives to God in prayer since time out of mind.

Boatmen of the Caldey 'pool', 1983 (from left to right): Raymond Thomas; Charles Crockford; Bing Jones; Les Day; David Crockford; Jim Crockford; Teddy Richards; Nicky Crockford; Alan Thomas; Brian Bolton; Gabriel Cummins; Father Stephen; Freddie Lewis.

8 Natural History

It remains only to say something of the natural history of the islands, although much of it has always been, as it must always be, related to the presence of man and his activities.

The coming of the internal combustion engine, for example, with its attendant and insidious discharge of waste oil, has had an incalculable effect, not only on the sea-birds themselves, but on the marine food on which they depend. A lack of farming operations has resulted in changes in vegetation, most notably on Skomer, as the ubiquitous bracken steadily takes over along with the brambles and nettles.

It was man who introduced rabbits to the islands and it is man who, down through the centuries, has either profited from their presence or suffered from their depredations, and has tried to control them or to exterminate the creatures. The rabbit disease myxomatosis caused a spectacular crash in the rabbit populations in 1954 and 1955. Since then recoveries have been followed by further outbreaks as the numbers have built up and the disease has become attenuated with each outbreak. On Caldey, however, man interfered, and after the last outbreak it was possible to locate and destroy the survivors.

Rats, either from trading ships or from straw and fodder brought from mainland farms, have colonised Ramsey and Caldey.

There are mice on Skokholm, introduced by rabbit-trappers in the 1890s, and Skomer has its colony of voles, but there are no predators such as foxes, stoats and weasels on any of the islands.

The rats, inevitably, have had a marked effect on the sea-bird colonies and have driven the nocturnal shearwaters and the puffins from Caldey and Ramsey. Both these species still nest in the rabbit burrows and the cliff-top holes on Skomer and Skokholm. These two islands also have their populations of storm petrels, and St Margaret's is notable for its large breeding colony of cormorants. These great black enemies of fisherman are essentially estuarine feeders and the whole of Carmarthen Bay is a happy hunting ground for them. The reason for this is not far to seek. The bay contains many estuaries and is itself shallow, much of it having, until comparatively recent times in history, been forest and lowland.

It is perhaps an interesting thought that, whilst the emphasis is now on study and conservation, the interest is such that increasing numbers of people have to be encouraged to visit in order to provide the money for wardening, and thereby cause more disturbance than those, far fewer in number, who have in times past gone about their daily tasks of farming Pembrokeshire's islands.

Further reading
This work has been based almost entirely on the author's own books: *Cliffs of Freedom* (Llandysul), 1961; *The Sounds Between* (Llandysul), 1968; *Across the Sounds* (Llandysul), 1972; *Total Community* (Tenby), 1975 and (Llandysul), 1994; *Caldey* (Llandysul), 1984, and *Farewell the Islands* (Llandysul), 1987, in all of which full bibliographical references will be found.